I Like Giving.

THE 7 WAYS OF LIVING GENEROUSLY

Give, share, and show you care.

GENEROUS THOUGHTS: Use a thought in my mind to think something kind.

GENEROUS WORDS: Use what I say to make someone's day.

GENEROUS MONEY: Use my money — no matter how much — if there is a life I can touch.

GENEROUS TIME: Use any moment in my day to put Generosity on display.

GENEROUS INFLUENCE: Use the choices that I make to affect the actions other people take.

GENEROUS ATTENTION: Use my eyes to look and ears to hear. Listen well and distractions disappear.

GENEROUS BELONGINGS: Use what I have to share — I can do this anywhere.

Leroy the Lion and the Incredible Influence

Copyright © 2024 by I Like Giving.®

Author Betta Tugive is the pen name for the I Like Giving.® Writing Team.

Scriptures taken from the Holy Bible, New International Version®, NIV®. Copyright © 1973, 1978, 1984, 2011 by Biblica, Inc.™ Used by permission of Zondervan. All rights reserved worldwide. www.zondervan.com. The "NIV" and "New International Version" are trademarks registered in the United States Patent and Trademark Office by Biblica, Inc.™

All rights reserved. No part of this book may be reproduced or transmitted in any form or by any means, electronic or mechanical, including photocopying and recording, or by information storage or retrieval system, without permission in writing from I Like Giving.®

Printed in the United States of America 2024.

ISBN 979-8-9897198-3-9

**Dedicated to Doodle —
a generous influence and friend.**

I Like Giving.® Writing Team:
S.F. Aughtmon
and friends

Illustrated by
Ben Cole & Andy Towler

Special thanks to Kirsti and Mike

The Giving Adventure Series

**Jasper G and the
Me-Thinking Madness**

**Ellie the Elephant and the
Stinkin' Thinkin'**

**Polly the Parrot and the
Wonderful Words**

**Marco the Monkey and the
Marvelous Money**

**Stanley the Sloth and the
Tremendous Timekeeper**

**Leroy the Lion and the
Incredible Influence**

LEROY THE LION
AND THE
INCREDIBLE INFLUENCE

BY

Betta Tugive

I Like Giving. Publishing
Colorado Springs, CO

In the land of the givers, where kindness is king, lived a lion named Leroy, and art was his thing.

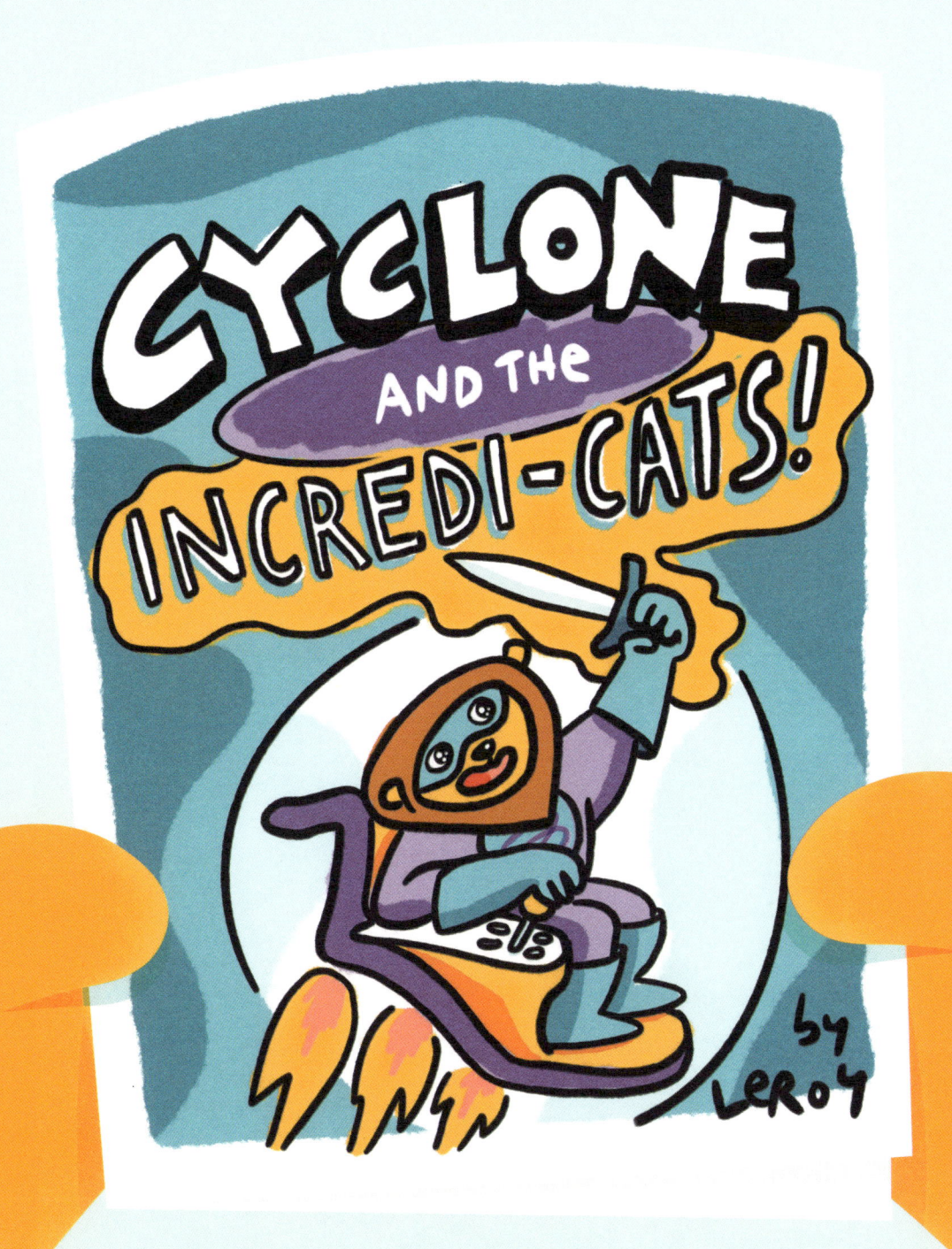

Leroy showed his friend, Polly, his latest cartoon, with a hero on wheels who could zoom to the moon.

STUDENT BY DAY...

"He's a lion named Lewis who fights against fear.
And he turns into Cyclone when evil is near!"

"But when Cyclone is cornered and needs a big win,
then he calls all the other INCREDI-CATS in.
With their smarts and their powers, they know what to do.
Lions help one another. They always come through!"

"Oh, I like how your Cyclone can zip through the air.
You have drawn all your comics with fun and with flair."

"Everyone in my family's creative, you know. Yes, they paint or they sculpt or they make pots to show."

"Our whole crew's meeting up at the Show-Your-Art tent. The museum is hosting this special event."

"It's a cartoon convention with cool Chuck Le Chat!
He's a big animator and artistic cat."

MEET CHUCK LE CHAT!

"He'll be showing his comics. They'll be on display. Chuck is meeting and greeting his fans the same day."

Oh, I love Chuck Le Chat, and I'm such a big fan! I would love to go see him, and that was my plan.

But I looked everywhere, and the tickets were gone.

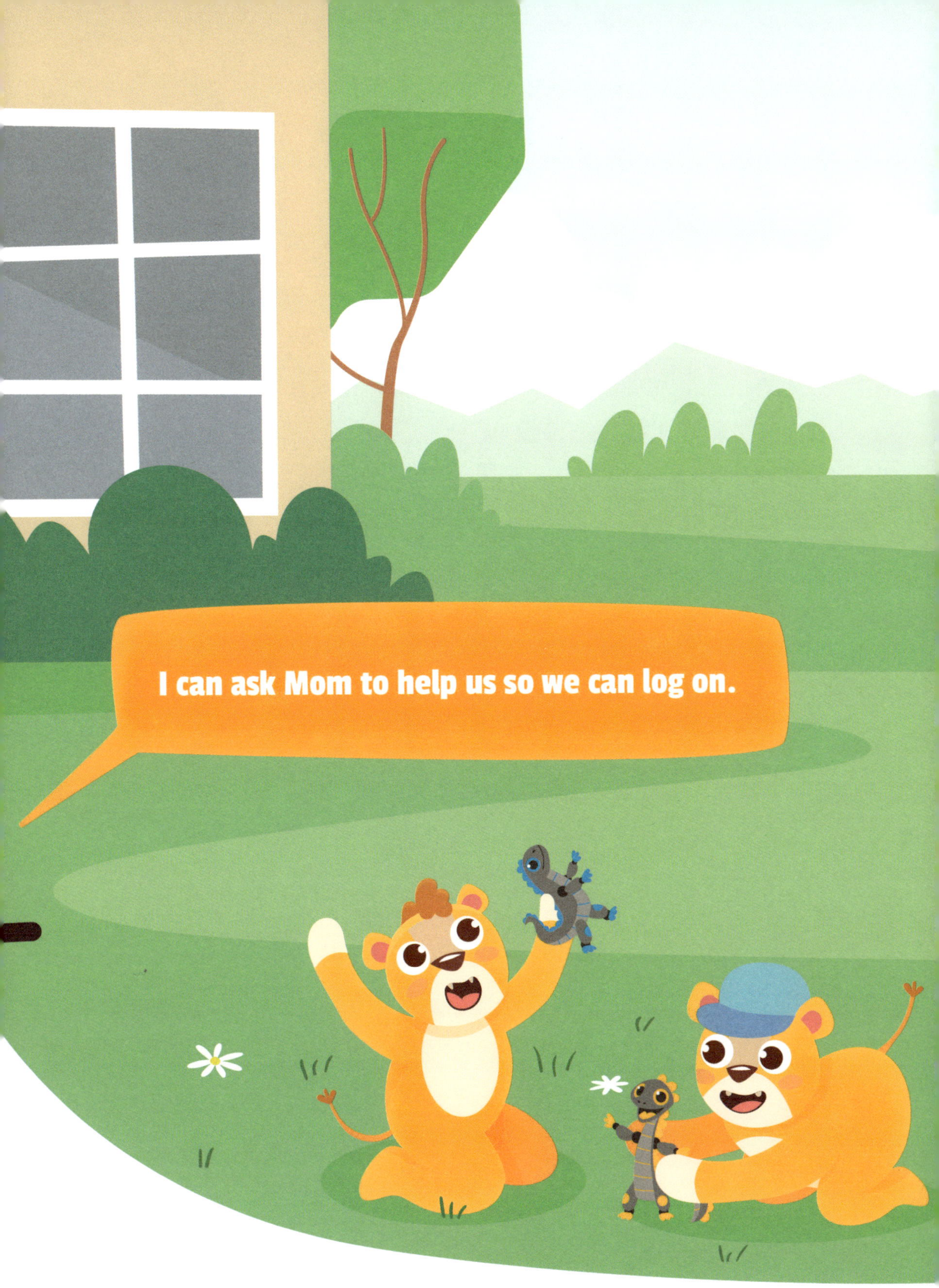
I can ask Mom to help us so we can log on.

The pals searched every site,

    and they looked high and low.

But they couldn't find tickets for Polly to go.

Leroy thought with his thinker,

Now what should I do?
I think Polly should meet up with Chuck Le Chat too.
If my heroes were here, I know they'd save the day.
They would all work together and find a new way.

Then a wonderful thought filled his thinker with glee —
What about the fun heroes who live next to me?

"I can help save the day with a crew of my own!
I've got cats upon cats upon cats that I've known."

"We can go door to door down my whole family row,
and you'll meet the incredible lions I know."

"They've got smarts.

    They're inspiring.

        They'll know what to do.

Lions help one another. I know they'll come through."

The friends knocked on each door — Leroy talked to his aunts. And his cousins. His grandma. His uncle from France.

"Say, do you have a ticket to see Chuck Le Chat?
'Cuz my friend Polly needs one, and we need it stat!"

At the very last house on the end of the street, lived his great-great-great-uncle, Lorenzo Petite. The small lion was known for his ginormous heart.

"Can you help us get in to see Chuck Le Chat's art?"

"No, I don't have a ticket,
　　but here's what I'll do.
I can share a great friend
　　who'd love chatting with you."

And then who should step out of the door on the mat?

The incredible artist himself...

CHUCK Le CHAT!

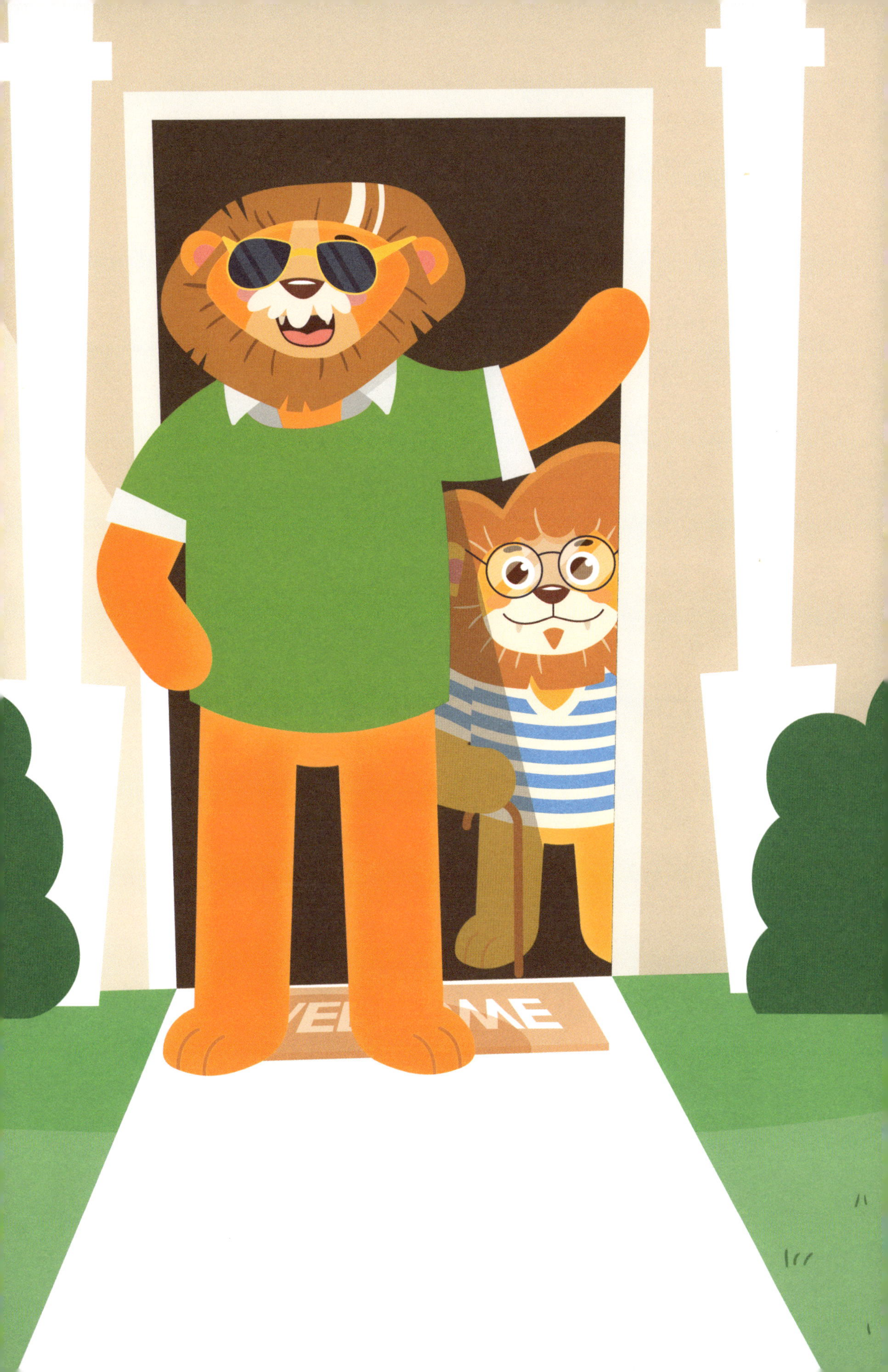

"You see, Chuck is my pal.
    We met way back in school.
And he thinks hanging out
    with young artists is cool.
Would you like to come in?
    Sharing friends is the best!"

When we learn from each other, we're happy and blessed!

The new pals had a blast,
young and old, side by side,
sharing comics and drawings
and stories with pride!

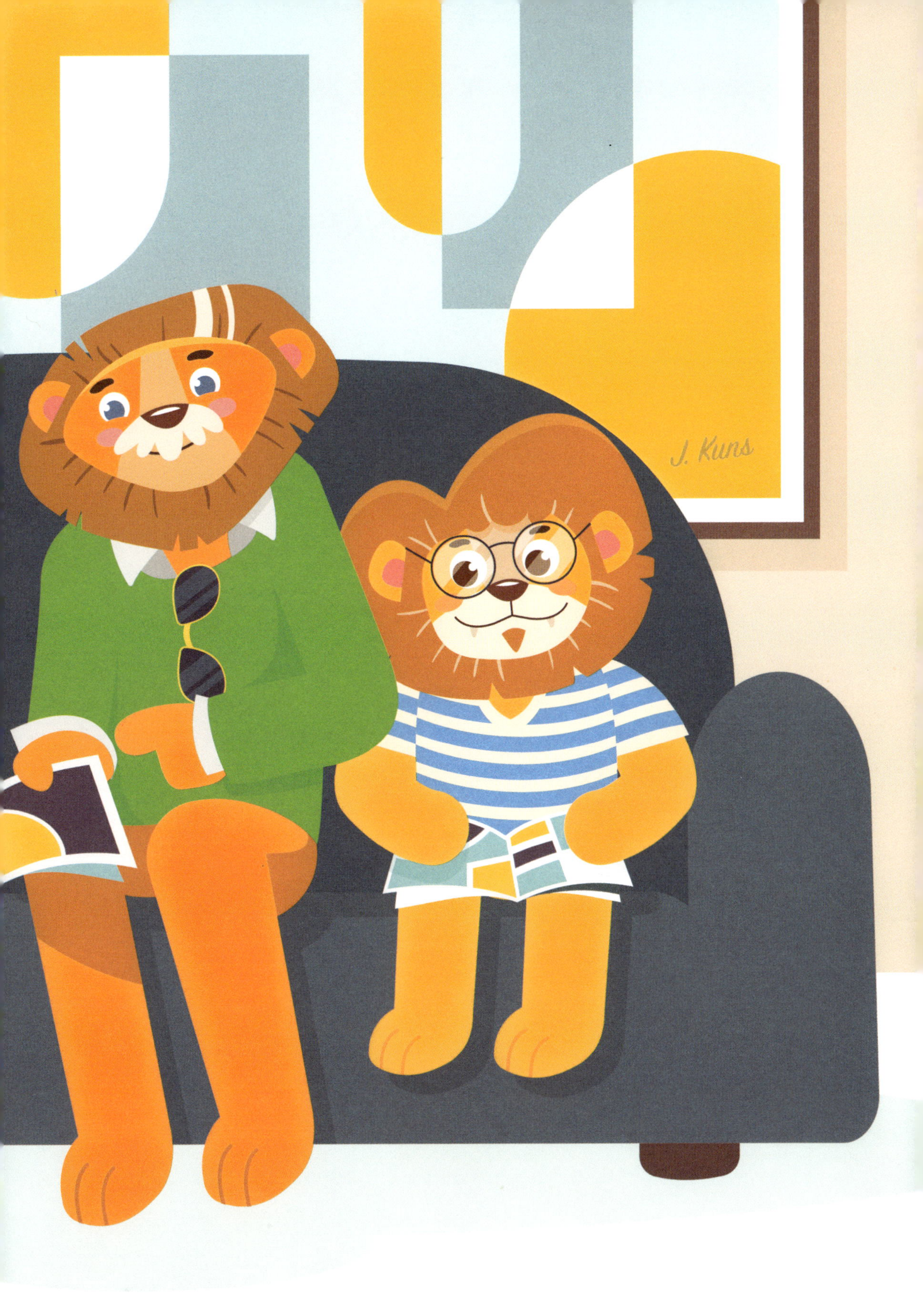
J. Kuns

I had such a great time.
I don't want it to end!
Your whole family is cool,
and we met a new friend.

Well, who knew that connecting
could be such a blast?
And my cats upon cats?
They make friendships that last!

Say, do you know somebody who needs help from you?
Share your pals upon pals. Now you know what to do!

Use your Generous Influence — you'll be the one who will double your friendships with twice as much fun!

Talk About It & Put It Into Action!

Generous influence is the way you use your friendships, relationships, and connections to help someone else.

How did Leroy share his friendships to help Polly?

Family Connect Challenge

Think of two of your friends who you think would enjoy getting to know each other! Ask your parents to arrange a playdate so you all can play together!

More To Explore In The Digital Portal!

View the e-book animation, family activities, coloring pages, and more!

So in everything, do to others what you would have them do to you.
Matthew 7:12 (NIV)

GENEROUS STUDENTS
HOMESCHOOL EDITION

Join the Generosity Road Trip! **Generous Students™: Homeschool Edition** explores The 7 Ways of Living Generously for all age groups!

GENEROUS FAMILY

generousfamily.com

Check out our K-8 faith-based, biblical SEL curriculum! Generous Classroom™ is sharing the importance of gratitude and teaching the next generation how to be life-long givers!

K-2

3-5

6-8

GENEROUS CLASSROOM™

generousclassroom.com